21ST CENTURY SCIENCE

GLOBAL POLLUTION

By Rebecca Mileham

Publisher: Melissa Fairley
Editor: Miranda Smith
Designer: Emma Randall
Production Controller: Ed Green
Production Manager: Suzy Kelly

ISBN-13: 978-1-84898-106-5 pbk

Picture credits (t=top; b=bottom; c=centre; OFC= outside front cover; OBC=outside back cover):

Piyal Adhikary/epa/Corbis: 50–51. Pablo Bartholomew/Getty Images: 20t. Philippe Benoist/Look at Sciences/Science Photo Library: 41b. Martin Bond/Science Photo Library: 59b. Borderlands/Alamy: 38b. Chagai/Wikimedia Commons (PD):46–47. Anthony Cooper; Ecoscene/Corbis: 15t. Thomas Deerinck, NCMIR/Science Photo Library: 18t. ESA: 6–7. Fox Photos/Hulton Archive/Getty Images: 12t. Simon Fraser/Science Photo Library: 29t. Diego Giudice/Corbis: 39b. Brian K Grigsby, SPC5, Photographer, ARC Identifier 530626/NARA: 36–37t. Hidden Ocean 2005 Expedition/NOAA/Office of Ocean Exploration: 10, 11r. iStock: 8–9, 16–17t, 34–35b, 48b, 54l, 60–61. Kelly Cheng Travel Photography/Getty Images: 32–33. Martinkovic, P/US Fish and Wildlife Service: 5t. MODIS Rapid Response Team, Goddard Space Flight Center/NASA: 9t. NASA Scientific Visualization Studio Collection: 23b. Chad Naughton/National Science Foundation: 21t. NOAA Corps: 22t. Ria Novosti/Science Photo Library: 7t, 49t. David Nunuk/Science Photo Library: 44–45. Caroline Penn/Corbis: 24–25. Photodisc: 28t. Duncan Shaw/Science Photo Library: 11t. Shutterstock: OFC, 1 all, 2, 3 all, 4–5, 6l, 7r, 7r (background), 8l, 9r, 9r (background), 12l, 13 all, 14 all, 15r, 15r (background), 16–17t, 18l, 18b, 19 all, 20l, 21r, 22l, 23r, 26–27 all, 28l, 29r, 29r (background), 30–31 all, 33b, 34l, 34t, 35r, 35r (background), 36l, 37r, 37r (background), 40 all, 41r, 41r (background), 42l, 42t, 43 all, 46l, 47t, 47r, 47r (background), 48l, 49r, 49r (background), 52–53 (all), 54 all, 55r, 56–57, 58l, 59r, 59r (background), 60l, 61r, 62, 63, 64, OBC all. SunStang Solar Car Project/Wikimedia Commons (GNU 1.2): 58t.

Every effort has been made to trace copyright holders, and we apologize in advance for any omissions. We would be pleased to insert the appropriate acknowledgements in any subsequent edition of this publication.

NOTE TO READERS

The website addresses are correct at the time of publishing. However, due to the ever-changing nature of the Internet, websites and content may change. Some websites can contain links that are unsuitable for children. The publisher is not responsible for changes in content or website addresses. We advise that Internet searches are supervised by an adult.

ENVIRONMENTAL DISASTER

IN 1998, THE SEA WASHED UP A TURTLE ON A SCOTTISH BEACH. INSIDE ITS STOMACH, VETS FOUND 57KG OF PLASTIC BAGS THAT THE TURTLE HAD PROBABLY MISTAKEN FOR EDIBLE JELLYFISH. INSTEAD, THE PLASTIC BLOCKED AND DAMAGED ITS INTERNAL ORGANS. THE TURTLE IS ONLY ONE OF AN ESTIMATED 100,000 ANIMALS – MANY OF WHICH ARE BIRDS – THAT DIE EVERY YEAR FROM EATING OR GETTING TANGLED IN PLASTIC LITTER.

LITTER POLLUTION

Litter is a very visible example of pollution. If you are a litter lout, you now risk an on-the-spot fine in some towns and cities. This scheme is aimed at reducing the tide of trash that makes the streets, countryside and beaches dirty and dangerous.

POLLUTION AND THE ECOSYSTEM

Like other forms of pollution, litter is a problem that we are inflicting on ourselves. Pollution affects the air we breathe, the water we drink and the land on which we rely for food and survival. Since many of our planet's natural systems interconnect, pollution in one place soon turns up elsewhere. For example, if a farmer overuses **pesticides** on the land, the excess will wash into local rivers and streams, and could eventually cause problems in the sea. And the **carbon dioxide** given out, when for example cars burn **fossil fuels**, is carried around the world and contributes to **global warming**.

Different lifestyles around the world inflict different amounts of pollution on the environment. The way life is lived in countries in the West usually results in a bigger price tag for the planet. Economic growth in less developed places often goes hand-in-hand with a bigger environmental impact. But every one of the globe's residents – human, animal and plant – is affected in some way by pollution. And all six billion humans have a part to play in cleaning up the Earth.

This seagull has become entangled in plastic packaging and drowned. People need to dispose of their rubbish safely to avoid damaging wildlife.

WHAT IS POLLUTION?

Pollution describes the introduction of substances or energy by people that can cause hazards. These can be to human health, living resources and ecological systems, structures or services. The main areas are:

- air – the main causes of air pollution, traffic and industry
- water – pollution of drinking water, rivers and sea, and the causes of **acid rain**
- land – farming, manufacturing and pollution-related impact
- pollution in the home – the pollutants we encounter when cooking, eating or getting dressed
- pollution in the environment – light pollution, noise and **radiation**
- climate pollution – **climate change** and how pollution is affecting it.

The hawksbill turtle is a critically endangered sea turtle, threatened by human activities.

A WINDOW ON THE WORLD

In March 2002, people all over Europe held their breath as a rocket blasted off from French Guiana. Aboard was Europe's biggest and most expensive satellite. Called **Envisat**, it was carrying ten sensitive scientific instruments to monitor the environment. Envisat's creators hoped that their new tool would provide a window on the world, showing with incredible accuracy where pollution, human lifestyles, natural phenomena and disasters were impacting the planet. The launch went without a hitch, and Envisat started its first journey around Earth, completing one orbit every 100 minutes.

ICE COLLAPSE

Just over two weeks later, Envisat was in exactly the right place at the right time. The satellite's cameras captured the spectacular collapse and disintegration of the Larsen B ice shelf in Antarctica. This was the latest evidence of how atmospheric warming affects the Antarctic Peninsula, and triggered the break-up of ice shelves across the region. Scientists are still investigating the reasons behind the ice collapse – is human-made pollution entirely to blame for the atmospheric warming that caused it?

KEEPING TRACK OF POLLUTION

Not every sign of pollution's impact is easy to spot. If an ocean gets a tiny bit dirtier or a tiny bit warmer every day as a result of pollution, it may take years for

The hi-tech satellite Envisat is the largest Earth Observation spacecraft ever built. It monitors Earth's land, atmosphere, oceans and ice caps.

A worker wearing a protective suit sprays decontaminants on a building after the Chernobyl nuclear disaster in 1986.

the impact to become obvious. Radiation such as that released by the Chernobyl nuclear disaster was invisible, but its effects have been devastating and long-lasting. Envisat is the latest tool helping to show up the long-term effects that people are having on the planet. Instruments aboard the satellite can add together data from different trips to reveal how the planet is changing over time. And citizens, politicians and scientists are all taking the evidence seriously.

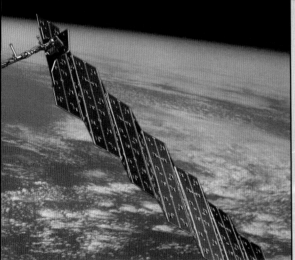

INVESTIGATING THE EVIDENCE: OBSERVING POLLUTION FROM SPACE

The investigation: The aim was to find out how much pollution people are producing, where it is in the atmosphere and how it is influencing climate change.

The scientists: John Burrows is the director of the Institute of Environmental Physics and Remote Sensing at the University of Bremen in Germany. He and his team at the European Space Agency (ESA) are working on the **Sciamachy** science instrument carried aboard Envisat.

Collecting the evidence: Sciamachy's job is to collect data to give a 3-D picture of the quantity, location and composition of gases in the atmosphere. To do this it collects and measures sunlight that is transmitted, reflected and scattered by the Earth's atmosphere or surface in the ultraviolet, visible and near infrared wavelengths.

The conclusion: Sciamachy has shown that pollution, which is mainly produced in the lower atmosphere, is moved around by the wind, affecting all of the Earth. The amounts are increasing in proportion to population growth and increases in standards of living.

FUMES, FUEL AND FRIDGES

Coke plants overshadow the town of Tangshan, China, belching fumes as they churn out fuel for the country's steel industry. Town residents complain of skin and breathing problems, heart disease and even cancer. Officials shut down plants during the 2008 Beijing Olympics – but only for a while. The standard of living for many of China's 1.3 billion people is increasing, giving better access to the cars, fridges and washing machines taken for granted elsewhere. But the demand for steel is adding to a huge pollution problem.

POLLUTION AND WEALTH

It is a similar story in Tehran, Iran's capital city. In the last 20 years, the city's population has grown to 14 million, with an estimated 2 million cars on the roads. The cost is in the pollution levels that contribute to about 5,000 deaths every year. When the **smog** reaches danger level, schools close. Some European cities experience similar problems. Smog regularly hits northern Italian cities when fumes from traffic and heating systems build up in dry weather.

Air pollution in Beijing is becoming a dangerous health hazard.

TAKING ACTION

Italian authorities have experimented with traffic bans, encouraging people to travel by bicycle or on rollerblades. Iran's leaders have pledged to phase out dirty cars and tackle the

INVESTIGATING THE EVIDENCE: CHINESE SMOG

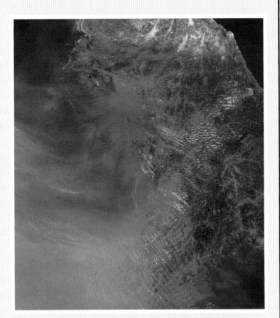

The polluted air created by industry in China can be clearly seen in this satellite photo.

pollution problem in all the country's big cities. And in Tangshan, China, campaigners are positive that increased media reports of pollution problems will eventually result in action about their dirty coke factory.

The investigation: A scientific team conducted research to find out how China's recent and rapid industrial development is affecting the country's climate and air quality.

The scientists: A team from the US Department of Energy, led by Climate Physics Scientist Yun Qian of the Pacific Northwest National Laboratory in Washington State, USA.

Collecting the evidence: Yun Qian and his team studied records from over 500 weather stations across China covering the last 50 years. They examined the records for information on the levels of solar radiation (the heat from the Earth's surface caused by sunshine) and the number of clear or cloudy days. Using this data, they made climate models to better understand the impact of pollution.

The conclusion: China is significantly darker than it was 50 years ago. The country has reduced solar radiation, despite the fact that there are more clear days. This is because of the existence of atmospheric smog, which is caused by fossil fuel pollution, the researchers say. Emissions have also increased by nine times over the last 50 years. And this, in turn, is increasing the likelihood of acid rain and respiratory diseases.

CHAPTER ONE

A MODERN PROBLEM?

THE PROBLEM OF POLLUTION WAS AROUND LONG BEFORE MODERN FACTORIES WERE BUILT. NASTY FUMES AND POISONOUS PARTICLES WERE AN ISSUE IN ANCIENT TIMES – AND THE CLUES ARE STILL AROUND FOR US TO FIND. THERE IS EVIDENCE OF COPPER AND LEAD POLLUTION IN OLD MINING AREAS THAT DATES RIGHT BACK TO THE BRONZE AGE.

CLUES IN THE ICE

Columns of ice that are being dug up in Greenland can give a snapshot of the chemical content of the Earth's climate that dates back nearly 8,000 years. By analyzing **ice cores** that measure up to 1km in length, the scientists have found that the number of lead particles trapped in the ice increased at dates that correspond directly to the rise of the powerful Greek and Roman empires.

Peat mosses absorb pollutants from the air. Samples taken from 10m down in a peat bog can reveal these pollutants.

ANCIENT POLLUTION

Experts believe the source of lead pollution was the existence of ancient silver factories, in which people smelted lead ore to extract the valuable metal. The Greeks first employed this technique on a large scale, and used the proceeds to finance their victories in war. Roman silver production was even more widespread. The Roman Empire's lead pollution rivalled that produced by early modern factories. Some research indicates that lead poisoning may have affected the mental and physical health of wealthy Romans and helped to speed the end of the Roman Empire.

In Alaska, a scientist takes one ice core (centre), while another measures a second (foreground).

HISTORY IN ICE, WATER AND SOIL

If scientists can track pollution levels from the past – both recent and long ago – this can help them to work out the likely future effect of today's pollution. As well as the information they get from ice cores, they also investigate the **sediments** that collect at the bottom of lakes. This provides a rich source of information on the pollutants that have affected the water over a period of years. **Peat** bogs offer another way of finding out about pollution's history. Mosses growing in the bog live by absorbing **nutrients** from the air, but they absorb pollutants at the same time. These pollutants are buried in the layers of peat and the geologists are able to date them.

A tugboat makes its way up the River Thames near Tower Bridge in heavy smog in 1952.

TOURIST ATTRACTIONS

If you visit London as a tourist today, you will probably make a point of seeing the Houses of Parliament and the London Eye. But in the 19th century, visitors often came to see London for a very different reason. During cold weather, the city would often be gripped by a yellow-black blanket of smoky fog or 'smog'. The city became famous for its so-called 'pea-soupers'.

THE INDUSTRIAL REVOLUTION

The **Industrial Revolution** saw factories open up all over Britain, powered by steam from coal-fired boilers. Smogs occurred during calm weather, when low wind speeds meant that pollutants were trapped in still air near ground level. In the winter, people burned extra coal for heat, adding to the smoke and sulphur dioxide pollution from the factories nearby. Respiratory problems claimed many lives.

THE DOWNSIDES OF CHANGE

There are positives and negatives associated with the Industrial Revolution. Today, in countries where life is more basic, people are striving to embrace the changes that made such a difference to life in Britain, the USA and other western countries. Whatever the benefits of such economic development, there is no denying

▶▶ www.sciencemuseum.org.uk/visitmuseum/galleries/energy_hall.aspx

that it comes at a price. While the overall standard of living may increase, it is often on the back of thousands of low-paid workers – sometimes including children. Mines and factories have left behind tracts of land contaminated with poisonous by-products of industry. Levels of the gas carbon dioxide, blamed for climate change, have been higher in the atmosphere since the start of the Industrial Revolution. And some streams and rivers are still showing the effects of the acid rain caused by Industrial Revolution pollution.

Llama dung has been used to reduce the acid content of water leaking from mines in Bolivia.

INVESTIGATING THE EVIDENCE: CAN LLAMA DROPPINGS CLEAN UP POLLUTION?

The investigation: Scientists wanted to solve the problem of toxic elements such as cadmium that were leaking from disused tin and silver mines in Bolivia and polluting the main water supplies in the region. The idea was to use waste materials to treat the polluted mine waters.

The scientists: Professor Paul Younger of Newcastle University School of Civil Engineering and Geosciences, UK, and a local engineer in Bolivia, Marcos Arce.

Collecting the evidence: During a five-month trial, the scientists used a series of tanks to mix the mine water with limestone and readily available llama dung. The mixture absorbed the high levels of acid in the water leaking from the mine, while the dung helped to neutralize the acid.

The conclusion: The llama dung worked well and the water acidity dropped dramatically, as Professor Younger had hoped. He had previously carried out trials on mines in the north of England using cow and horse dung.

13

Today, many industrial activities cause pollution of air, land and water. It is essential that governments work towards controlling this potential threat to our planet.

A GLOBAL AGREEMENT

In 1990, ministers from countries across the world met in Kyoto, Japan, to talk tough on climate issues. The outcome was the Kyoto Protocol, a historic commitment to reducing **greenhouse-gas** emissions. By 2009, 183 nations had ratified the agreement. Under the protocol, industrialized countries have agreed to reduce their collective emissions of greenhouse gases by just over five per cent compared to the year 1990. The issues are not easy, but the protocol is one of the ways in which countries are starting to work together to tackle environmental problems.

LAWS AND CHANGE

Kyoto is an international protocol, so it cannot be enforced like a law. And some campaigners believe that its measures are too little, too late, to rescue us from the global warming that could mean disaster in many regions. But legal solutions have often helped control pollution in countries where laws catch up with technological developments. The UK government enforced the Clean Air Act following the Great Smog that hit London for four months in early 1953. The dirty fog was so bad that cinemas and theatres closed because

▶ ▶ http://unfccc.int/2860.php

Upland streams, like this in the Brecon Beacons in the UK, were monitored for sulphur pollution (right).

INVESTIGATING THE EVIDENCE: ACID RAIN RECOVERY IN THE UK

The investigation: A team of scientists investigated how the UK's rivers and waterways are coping against the effects of acid rain. The team's aim is to apply their expertise in aquatic science, and their knowledge of the effects of human impact on the aquatic ecosystems, to environmental problem-solving.

The scientists: A team from the Environmental Change Research Centre (ECRC) at University College, London, that was led by Professor Rick Battarbee.

Collecting the evidence: The scientists monitored 22 sites in lakes and streams in the upland areas of the UK. They measured the acidity of the water and the levels of polluting sulphur.

The conclusion: Acidity has halved over the last 15 years and many species of plants and animals have reappeared. One major reason for the improvement is the addition of new technology to remove sulphur from the emissions that come out of two large British power stations.

audiences could not see the screen or stage! Doctors attributed 12,000 deaths to the smog. Modern clean-air legislation came into force in the USA in 1963, although cities such as Chicago and Cincinnati already had legal controls on atmospheric pollution in place.

A CLEANER ACT

The UK's clean air laws forced factories and home-owners to use cleaner fuel for power and heating. As a result, by 2005, many rivers, lakes and streams had started to recover from the effects of acid rain caused by dirty fuels. In particular, a switch from coal to natural gas helped to halve the sulphur in the water and boosted populations of fish, plants and insects.

 # BREATHE EASIER!

WITH QUEUES OF BELCHING LORRIES, CARS AND BUSES, URBAN ROADS DO NOT SEEM THE MOST ATTRACTIVE OR CLEANEST PLACES TO TAKE A WALK. BUT RECENT RESEARCH HAS REVEALED THAT FAR FROM BEING THE WORST OPTION, WALKING ACTUALLY EXPOSES PEOPLE TO LESS POLLUTION THAN IF THEY TRAVELLED BY BUS OR TAXI.

TRACKING POLLUTION

Results like this are helping scientists understand and track traffic pollution. Vehicle engines are responsible for a cocktail of pollutants that damage people's health and harm the environment. They include **carbon monoxide, nitric oxide**, volatile organic compounds, **particulate matter** (particles small enough to breathe in), and in countries using leaded petrol, lead. Each engine emits a small amount of each pollutant, but the quantities add up. Across the world, experts predict a billion cars will be crowding onto the roads by 2020.

CUTTING THE HUMAN COST

Outdoor air pollution harms more than 1.1 billion people, mostly in cities. The World Health Organization (WHO) estimates that about 700,000 deaths annually could be prevented in developing countries if carbon monoxide, particulate matter and lead were reduced. There is some good news – all southern African countries are now committed to converting to unleaded fuel, leaving only some north African and Asian nations to catch up.

The benefits of more efficient engines – and the use of less atmospheric pollutants – tend to be cancelled out by the increases in the numbers of vehicles that run on the roads.

AIR DAMAGE

Even before a baby is born, pollution is at work in their developing body. Air pollution can damage children's lungs while they grow in the womb, according to the World Health Organization. The pollutants responsible are particulates, fine particles in the air from natural sources such as sea spray and human activities such as burning fossil fuels. When these fragments are smaller than 10 microns across (a fifth of the width of a human hair), they are known as PM10. The nose cannot filter them out, so PM10 particulates can penetrate into a mother's lungs – potentially damaging her baby.

These are the microscopic particulates given out by the exhaust fumes of cars.

POLLUTION SOURCES

The main culprit in this pollution example is not traffic pollution, as you might expect. Since European children spend up to 90 per cent of their time indoors, their exposure to indoor sources of air pollution is very high. It is the solid fuel that many European households use for heating that is the main source of PM10 for children.

The WHO believes that the best way out of the problem is to encourage families to turn away from solid fuel towards cleaner liquid or gas fuels.

Indoor particulate pollution is responsible for more than a third of all deaths of under-4s in Europe, according to WHO figures. Illnesses include serious respiratory infections and asthma. Many more children end up in hospital with pneumonia. Outdoor particulates from traffic fumes play their part as well. Several thousand children die every year from associated respiratory tract infections, asthma, low birth weight and lungs that do not work properly. But if levels of these polluting particles could be reduced to EU guideline levels of 40 micrograms per cubic metre, more than 5,000 lives could be saved.

Solid fuels include wood, charcoal, coal and peat. These fuels give off particulates that can damage our health.

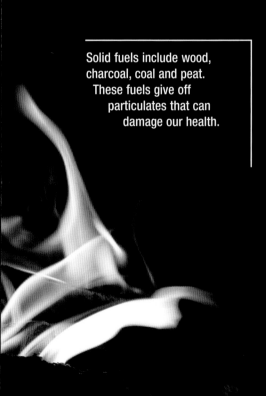

INVESTIGATING THE EVIDENCE: POLLUTION CAN DAMAGE CHILDREN'S LUNGS

The investigation: In the longest-ever study on air pollution and children's health, researchers tracked children over a ten-year period to learn the effects of air pollution on the health of their lungs.

The scientists: Dr John Peters and his team at the University of the Southern California Keck School of Medicine, USA.

Collecting the evidence: In the Children's Health Study, the scientists tested the respiratory function of more than 3,000 teenagers who they had also monitored when younger. Each year, they made each child take a deep breath, then measured how much and how fast they could blow out the air.

The conclusion: Children's lung function usually grows steadily until they reach adulthood. Those children who had grown up in the most polluted areas had less than 80 per cent of the lung function expected for their age. High levels of air pollution – from car exhausts and fossil-fuel burning – increase the risk of poor lung development by five times. The risk is second only to that of smoking. So far, the team do not know exactly how air pollution harms lungs, but they believe inflammation in response to daily pollution may play a role.

The explosion at the Union Carbide pesticide factory in Bhopal, India, in 1984 caused the deaths of 500,000 people.

DEADLY LEAK

On the night of 2 December 1984, a pesticide factory in Bhopal, India, began to leak a deadly gas. An incredible 27 tonnes of poisonous methyl isocyanate escaped from the plant, spreading quickly through the city and exposing half a million men, women and children to its effects. Thousands of people died immediately as their lungs filled with the poisonous gas. Since the accident, 15,000 more have died and 120,000 others are still suffering from serious health problems that are associated with the leak.

RESPONSIBILITY

The fallout from Bhopal's tragedy continues today. In 1999, tests on groundwater and well-water near the site of the accident showed levels of the poisonous element mercury were still thousands of times higher than is safe. The water also contained other chemicals that can cause cancers, birth defects and brain damage. Union Carbide, the company who owned the pesticide factory, was charged with causing the leak, but the company refused to appear in the Indian courts to answer the case. Often called the 'worst industrial disaster in history', the Bhopal chemical leak is an extreme

Gas bubbles trapped in ice store information about air pollution for thousands of years.

example of industrial pollution. But factories and power plants across the world release pollutants every day as they make the products and supply the energy demanded by the world's population.

FACTORY POLLUTION

Recent evidence from ice cores taken in Antarctica shows that the levels of greenhouse gases in the Earth's atmosphere are higher now than they have been for the last 650,000 years. And, alarmingly, the figures are rising faster than ever before. Factories are one of the major contributors to these levels. Sulphur emissions from burning fossil fuels are also contributing to the problem of acid rain.

A CAREER IN SCIENCE

Thomas Stocker is Professor of Climate and Environmental Physics at the University of Bern, Switzerland. Professor Stocker studied environmental physics at degree and postgraduate level, and has held university posts in Zurich, London, Montreal, New York and Honolulu, Hawaii.

A DAY IN THE LIFE OF ...

As one of the leaders of the ice-core drilling project EPICA, in Antarctica, Thomas Stocker is looking for evidence of changes in the amount of greenhouse gases in the Earth's atmosphere. The team is part of an international effort to drill into the ice to reveal climate gases trapped in tiny bubbles as the ice formed. They have drilled to a depth of 3,000m, looking back in time more than 800,000 years.

THE SCIENTIST SAYS ...

"One of the most important things is that we can put current levels of carbon dioxide and methane into a long-term context. We find that CO_2 is about 30 per cent higher than at any time, and methane 130 per cent higher ... and the rates of increase are absolutely exceptional: for CO_2, more than 100 times faster than at any time in the last 800,000 years."

Scientists launch an **ozonesonde** at the South Pole Station on Antarctica. The balloon-transported instrument measures a vertical profile of the **ozone** layer.

RECORD-BREAKING HOLES

While holiday-makers lounged on the beach in the summer of 2006, scientists were tracking one of the biggest-ever holes in the ozone layer. The hole, which opens over Antarctica each year, grew to twice the size of Europe, eventually covering an area of over 20 million square kilometres. It is the largest on record so far.

FRIDGES DAMAGE THE OZONE LAYER

The ozone layer is a protective blanket for Earth, saving the planet from harmful ultraviolet light from the Sun. It is up in the stratosphere – a region of Earth's atmosphere in which airliners fly because it is not turbulent. Damage to the Earth's ozone layer first came to light in the 1980s, and scientists identified the culprit as the tongue-twisting **chlorofluorocarbons (CFCs)** that are used as the coolant in fridges and air-conditioning units. These entirely artificial chemicals had only been around for 50 years. However, their impact on the planet had already been huge. CFCs were breaking up in the stratosphere, releasing chlorine atoms that could each destroy thousands of the ozone molecules that are protecting our planet.

▶▶ www.wmo.int/pages/prog/arep/gaw/ozone/index.html

OZONE HOLE SLOW-DOWN?

Scientists realized that ozone depletion meant an increased risk of skin cancer. Plants and animals were also affected by the change in radiation levels. Worried by this development, world leaders put the Montreal Protocol in place in 1987. This limited the use of CFCs and related chemicals. Although the protocol has been very successful, there is a new problem. Colder polar winters over the last few decades have increased ozone loss again. Scientists are keeping a close eye on what happens next.

In 2003, the ozone hole over Antarctica was larger than the North American continent, as can be seen in this computer model.

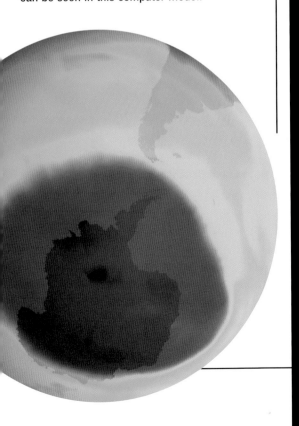

A CAREER IN SCIENCE

Geir Braathen is Senior Scientific Officer for the World Meteorological Organization (WMO) in Geneva, Switzerland. He studied chemistry, specializing in molecular spectroscopy (using frequencies to determine the make-up of chemical molecules). He worked in California, USA, before moving to the Norwegian Institute for Air Research.

A DAY IN THE LIFE OF ...

Geir is an expert in tracking ozone loss. He and his colleagues at the WMO use atmospheric data, much of which is collected using ozonesondes -- lightweight monitors for ozone and pressure, temperature and humidity. These are carried up into the stratosphere on balloons above the Arctic and Antarctic. They also use data sent from the Scanning Imaging Absorption Spectrometer for Atmospheric Chartography (Sciamachy) on board the ESA satellite Envisat.

THE SCIENTIST SAYS ...

"Although the levels of ozone-depleting substances are falling, there will still be damage to the ozone layer for many years to come. Colder than average temperatures in the stratosphere are also to blame for the ozone hole's unusually large recent size."

CHAPTER THREE

NOTHING TO DRINK

IN THE WEST AFRICAN COUNTRY OF MALI, HALF OF THE 11 MILLION PEOPLE HAVE NO ACCESS TO CLEAN WATER. NOWHERE IS THIS MORE SERIOUS THAN IN THE SLUMS SURROUNDING THE CAPITAL CITY BAMAKO. IN OVERCROWDED AND UNPLANNED SETTLEMENTS SUCH AS THESE, THERE IS NO RUNNING WATER, NOR ARE THERE SEWERS OR PROPER TOILETS. MAKESHIFT LATRINES OFTEN FILL QUICKLY AND OVERRUN, POLLUTING THE WATER IN THE SHALLOW, HAND-DUG WELLS.

A group of villagers in Gabulig Tingit, Ghana, Africa, carry containers holding rubble during the construction of a WaterAid well in their village.

CLEAN WATER ON TAP

In Bamako, the international charity WaterAid has shown that action is possible. They have financed an infrastructure to bring clean running water into the slums, then trained local people to maintain and operate the system. Money donated by members of the community has been enough to run the project as well as to invest in other development activities. With less time spent collecting water each day, more children are enrolling in schools. However, there is still plenty of work to do around the world. Waterborne diseases such as cholera, typhoid and dysentery kill one child every 15 seconds. And in Bangladesh, there is a problem with the wells that people rely on for their water – they are polluted with arsenic. The government drilled millions of deep new wells in the 1970s, so that people no longer had to drink contaminated surface water. But arsenic has been finding its way from the soil to the drinking water, causing cancers and painful lesions.

WATER SAVERS

This is all a reminder to us in the well-supplied West that clean water is a precious commodity. In developed countries, we can do a lot to avoid wasting water – from turning off the tap while cleaning our teeth to fitting a water-saving device in the toilet cistern so that it does not use as much water every time it is flushed. This is a drop in the ocean to those who live in the West.

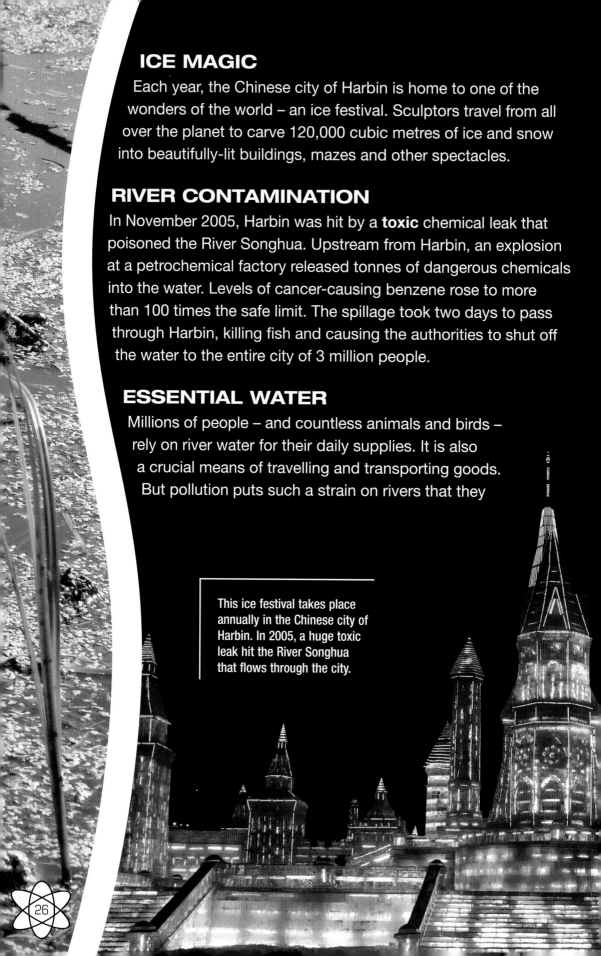

ICE MAGIC

Each year, the Chinese city of Harbin is home to one of the wonders of the world – an ice festival. Sculptors travel from all over the planet to carve 120,000 cubic metres of ice and snow into beautifully-lit buildings, mazes and other spectacles.

RIVER CONTAMINATION

In November 2005, Harbin was hit by a **toxic** chemical leak that poisoned the River Songhua. Upstream from Harbin, an explosion at a petrochemical factory released tonnes of dangerous chemicals into the water. Levels of cancer-causing benzene rose to more than 100 times the safe limit. The spillage took two days to pass through Harbin, killing fish and causing the authorities to shut off the water to the entire city of 3 million people.

ESSENTIAL WATER

Millions of people – and countless animals and birds – rely on river water for their daily supplies. It is also a crucial means of travelling and transporting goods. But pollution puts such a strain on rivers that they

This ice festival takes place annually in the Chinese city of Harbin. In 2005, a huge toxic leak hit the River Songhua that flows through the city.

are often unable to cope. Less than one per cent of the world's water is fresh and available for us to use. The rest is frozen into the polar ice caps, or sitting saltily in the oceans.

Sewage is the biggest problem for rivers when it is discharged in an untreated or semi-treated form. Food waste, excess pesticides and fertilizers from farmland as well as chemical outputs from industry also place a huge burden on our rivers and streams. Many of these types of pollution encourage bacteria to grow, eating up the river's natural oxygen and harming its native species. And even if a factory discharges water that is clean but warm, it can upset the natural balance and kill the fish and plants.

A CAREER IN SCIENCE

A former rugby player for Wales, Sandy Brown studied environmental pollution and is now a Catchment Sensitive Farming (CSF) officer for Natural England, an organization that aims to conserve England's natural environment.

A DAY IN THE LIFE OF ...

Sandy Brown works with local landowners and farmers to protect and restore Bassenthwaite Lake in the Lake District, Cumbria. This area is a National Nature Reserve and home to ospreys and endangered species of fish. Phosphate from fertilizers and animal manures as well as loose soil entering the lake has harmed water quality and wildlife. Natural England aims to sort out the water quality by persuading people to use better treatment plants on farms and sewage treatment works, as well as sharing information and encouraging farmers and local businesses to care for the environment.

THE SCIENTIST SAYS ...

"We are all working towards better water and farmers have a crucial part to play. Since 2005, 97 per cent of Bassenthwaite farmers have worked with us to reduce soil loss from their land and manage fertilizer use. This is great news for our farmers, the future of our water quality and the environment."

Oil slicks from ships at sea or in coastal waters are frequent and very dangerous to marine wildlife. The worst spillages can affect whole ecosystems.

DISASTER AT SEA

On the evening of 31 January 2006, a ship that was travelling through the Baltic Sea leaked 20 tonnes of fuel oil into the sea off the coast of Estonia. The ship's identity has never been established. By the next afternoon, local people spotted the slick coming ashore – bringing hundreds of dead birds in its wake.

DIRTY SEAS

Experts fear that the Estonian oil spill put up to 12,000 birds at risk. These included many rare species, such as golden-eye ducks and long-tailed ducks. And yet, the spillage was small compared to others that have happened in the past. Famous disasters include the *Exxon Valdez*, a tanker that grounded off the Alaskan coast in 1989. Its spilled cargo of more than 38,000 tonnes of crude oil killed 250,000 sea birds, plus thousands of otters, hundreds of eagles and more than 20 whales.

Oceans make up more than 71 per cent of our blue planet's surface. They tend to feel infinitely large, but the impact of human activities is radically affecting the seas, as well as the creatures that rely on it for survival.

This guillemot was covered in crude oil after a tanker ran aground on the south coast of Wales.

UGLY SECRETS

Until the practice was outlawed in 1989, ships would dump up to six million tonnes of rubbish into the sea every year, including plastic, glass, tin, wood and food waste. Sewage is another of the sea's dirty secrets, with millions of litres flowing into coastal waters every day. Smelly and ugly, sewage carries bacteria and viruses that poison sea creatures. Chemicals used by farmers and waste from factories are washed into rivers, travelling downstream and reaching the sea. The effects of these pollutants may include distorted growth in shellfish and a slow-down in the breeding of marine creatures.

INVESTIGATING THE EVIDENCE: ARSENIC IN THE WATER

The investigation: Millions of villagers who live on the floodplains and in the deltas of southern Asia rely on shallow wells for their water as the surface water is contaminated. However arsenic is polluting the water from these wells in Bengal and Bangladesh and scientists want to know why.

The scientists: Professor Jon Lloyd and his team at Manchester University, working with scientists and researchers from Kalyani University in Bangladesh.

Collecting the evidence: The team took sediment samples from wells in West Bengal and analyzed them using techniques from mineralogy, geochemistry and microbiology. This was the first time all these scientific tests had been combined.

The conclusion: The team found that bacteria in the soil are stripping the arsenic out of the soil around wells and depositing it in the water. The organisms are most effective in situations where there is not much oxygen in the water, so one way to tackle the problem may be to bubble air through to stop the release of the arsenic.

RAIN LIKE LEMON JUICE

In its natural state, rain's **pH value** (measure of acidity) would be quite low – between 5 and 6. But when rain is polluted, the pH increases to 4 – and some rain has even been measured at pH 2, the same acidity as lemon juice. The effect on some forests is devastating, with leaves damaged, natural nutrients washed away and harmful substances such as aluminium released into the soil.

BUILDINGS UNDER THREAT

This acid rain is threatening some of the world's most famous buildings. The US Capitol Building, constructed partly of marble, is losing its smooth appearance because acid rain dissolves the marble's mineral structure and allows small silicate pieces to fall out. It is the same story in the historic Italian city of Florence, where urban air pollution reacts with ancient marble facades and makes them more vulnerable to acid rain attack. Unpolluted rain is always slightly acidic because of its reaction with natural oxides in the air. But when the air is polluted with clouds of nitrogen oxide from traffic fumes and sulphur dioxide from coal-burning, the acidity increases dramatically.

Acid rain has damaged these spruces in the Harz National Park in Germany.

The ancient marble facades on the buildings of Florence, in Italy, are being damaged by acid rain.

NOT IN MY BACK YARD

Because acid rain is usually caused by emissions from factories, one country's industry tends to lead to another country's acid rain. Britain's factory chimneys are responsible for at least 16 per cent of the acid rain that has fallen in Norway. More than 90 per cent of Norway's acid pollution comes from other countries.

INVESTIGATING THE EVIDENCE: SILENT FORESTS AND ACID RAIN

The investigation: In a recent study, scientists wanted to determine the effect of acid rain on the habitat and breeding of wild birds.

The scientists: Dr Ralph Hames and his team in the Laboratory of Ornithology at Cornell University, USA.

Collecting the evidence: Ralph Hames' team tracked a particular bird, the wood thrush, that has a beautiful song and lives in forests on mountain slopes in the eastern United States. A drop in the numbers of this species had been observed since the 1960s, but research until now has been focussed on habitat loss and destruction. To help collect the data on the wood thrush, the scientists enlisted a group of amateur birdwatchers to monitor the birds right across their habitat. The scientists were looking for a possible link between acid rain and impaired breeding behaviour.

The conclusion: Acid rain has caused a number of effects on trees – from the loss of pine needles and leaves, to their complete destruction. The result is that the wood thrushes have fewer insects to eat, are in more danger from predators and have had to change their nesting and roosting habits. However, Dr Hames says that this is only one of the threats to the birds.

CHAPTER FOUR

FARMING AND THE LAND

THE TOWN OF MOYNAQ IN UZBEKISTAN WAS ONCE A THRIVING PORT ON THE ARAL SEA. BUT FOR 20 YEARS, THE BOATS HAVE BEEN ABANDONED BECAUSE THE ARAL SEA HAS BEEN SHRINKING, AND WHAT WATER IS LEFT IS NOW HEAVILY POLLUTED WITH PESTICIDES AND FERTILIZERS.

POLLUTED DESERT

The rivers feeding the Aral Sea were diverted in the 1930s to irrigate land for cotton crops. In the near future, according to the latest research, the southern part of the sea will probably be gone altogether. Cotton farming still continues, and farmers use large quantities of chemicals in their crop production. The pesticides and fertilizers that have run into the sea for decades mean that

These beached and decaying boats at Moynaq in Uzbekistan are the sad remains of a fishing industry that once employed thousands.

the desert-like land left behind when the sea recedes is dangerously dirty. Local people lack fresh water and suffer high rates of some cancers and lung disease.

Intensive farming of food and other crops has been around for less than a century, but its impacts have been huge. New machinery, such as combine-harvesters, and chemicals, such as insecticides, fertilizers and herbicides, allow the world's farmers to achieve higher levels of production from the land than ever before. But he overuse of these potentially harmful chemicals – whose effects are often not visible for many years – has led to protests.

FOOD FOR THOUGHT

The organic food movement developed in response to consumers' demand for products that were free from artificial pesticides, herbicides and **genetically modified** organisms. In many parts of the world, major supermarkets now stock organic ranges. Farmers' markets are springing up across Europe, offering access to local produce, meat and other foods directly from the people who produce them.

A combine-harvester gathers cotton, which is farmed in many countries, mainly to be spun into a thread used for making clothing.

BREAST IS BEST?

Breast milk is best for your baby – at least, that is the message that doctors have been promoting for years. But now scientists are warning that particularly nasty pollutants could be present in breast milk in worrying quantities. They are called **POPs (persistent organic pollutants)**. In animals, they have been linked to birth defects and behaviour disorders.

CHEMICALS THAT WILL NOT GO AWAY

POPs are a group of stable, artificial organic chemicals, mostly developed for use in industry. They include polychlorinated biphenyls (PCBs), used in electronics, paints, plastics and glues, as well as dioxins from many sources. The pesticide DDT, which first caused

Toxic plastic chemicals that act like a synthetic female hormone may be present in canned food.

widespread concern and launched the US environmental movement, is also a POP.

The stability of POPs makes them extremely useful, but the fact that they are not broken down by most natural processes is creating a problem. Present at low levels in the environment, POPs accumulate in larger and larger quantities as

▶ ▶ www.malaria.org/teachingmodules/ddt.html

they rise up the food chain. Amounts in breast milk can therefore be much higher than background levels. Despite this finding, doctors still advise that the positive effects of breastfeeding outweigh any potential risk from POPs.

THE DIRTY DOZEN

In 2004, a United Nations (UN) treaty came into force outlawing 12 of the worst POPs, known as the 'dirty dozen'. Countries who have signed up to the so-called Stockholm Convention have agreed not to produce, use or sell POPs, and should also destroy stocks. An exception has been made for DDT, which is still valued in the fight against malaria and is used in a handful of countries worldwide.

DDT is sprayed inside houses to kill the mosquito that carries the disease malaria. The disease kills more than a million people every year.

INVESTIGATING THE EVIDENCE: BISPHENOL A – IS IT A POLLUTANT?

The investigation: Scientists noticed that laboratory mice kept in cages made with the plastic component bisphenol A suffered unexpected genetic damage. They decided to investigate whether the chemical was to blame.

The scientists: Dr Patricia Hunt and her team at Case Western Reserve University, Ohio, USA.

Collecting the evidence: The scientists discovered that a detergent had been used to wash the mice's water bottles and cages. The bottles then leached bisphenol A into the water they contained and from there into the mice. The cages also leaked the chemical. The team investigated whether bisphenol A caused genetic abnormalities by deliberately introducing more of the chemical to the mice over a period of years, and comparing the results to mice that had been kept away from it.

Conclusion: The team found that the genetic problems were dependent on the dose of the chemical received, and damage occurred within levels thought to occur in the environment. Further research is under way, because bisphenol A is used extensively in dental fillings, shatter-proof plastics and the coatings inside food cans.

A UH-1D helicopter from the 336th Aviation Company sprays the defoliation agent known as Agent Orange on a dense jungle area in July 1969, during the Vietnam War.

POLITICAL POISONING

If you had read this story in a spy thriller, it might have seemed far-fetched – but it is true. In September 2004, the leader of the Ukrainian opposition party, Viktor Yushchenko, fell ill and his appearance started to change. His skin became blistered and disfigured. Tests a few months later revealed that Yushchenko had been poisoned with TCDD, the most harmful **dioxin** known. Yushchenko won the presidency of his country despite this attack. But the dioxin poisoning he suffered is an extreme example of the potential danger of such POPs.

THE HISTORY OF DIOXINS

Dioxins have a long and often sad history. They are organic chemicals that are released into the air in both natural events such as forest fires and by incineration of waste. They are also the toxic by-products when many items are manufactured, including antiseptics, fungicides and herbicides. The most notorious dioxin used was the herbicide Agent Orange, which was sprayed on Vietnamese forests by US troops during the Vietnam War (1959–75). The aim was to clear leaf cover that allowed enemy soldiers to hide. But the effects of Agent Orange, which contained high levels of TCDD, also caused thousands of birth defects in children and health disorders

▶ ▶ www.epa.gov/history/topics/lovecanal/01.htm

among the Vietnamese people and US war veterans. The legacy of this policy continues today.

TOXIC WASTE

Dioxins were also one of the nasty pollutants that forced the 1978 evacuation of Love Canal in Niagara Falls, USA. The Hooker Chemical and Plastics Corporation bought part of an unfinished canal to use as a disposal site for toxic waste. Despite warnings, new housing and a school were later built directly over the toxic dump. Residents began to complain that their children were often ill. There was a high rate of cancer and birth defects. After a two-year campaign by local people, and scientific results that showed that residents were suffering **chromosome** damage from the leaking chemical pollution, the US government evacuated the entire area, relocating 800 families.

INVESTIGATING THE EVIDENCE: WAS PRESIDENT YUSHCHENKO POISONED?

The investigation: In early September, 2004, Ukrainian presidential candidate Viktor Yushchenko's appearance changed radically. He claimed he had been poisoned by government agents, but was dioxin poisoning to blame?

The scientist: Abraham Brouwer, professor of environmental toxicology at the Free University in Amsterdam, the Netherlands.

Collecting the evidence: Professor Brouwer analyzed blood samples taken from Yushchenko. He found levels of dioxin that were thousands of times higher than normal. They were, in fact, the second-highest levels ever recorded.

The conclusion: Brouwer's team narrowed down the poison to the dioxin TCDD (tetrachlorodibenzoparadioxin), the most harmful known dioxin and an ingredient of Agent Orange. As it was a single, pure chemical, Professor Brouwer concluded there was no way the poisoning could have occurred naturally.

CHAPTER FIVE

DEADLY FIREPOWER

NORPARKUO IS A MAASAI WOMAN WHO LIVES IN KAJIADO, KENYA. HER DAY STARTS AT 4AM WHEN SHE LIGHTS THE FIRE IN HER HOME TO MAKE BREAKFAST. DURING THE DAY SHE WILL SPEND HOURS AROUND THE FIRE, COOKING OR HEATING WATER FOR BATHING AND DRINKING. SHE COMPLETES ALL HER DAILY TASKS WITH HER BABY SON STRAPPED TO HER BACK IN THE TRADITIONAL WAY, AND SO THE TWO OF THEM BREATHE SMOKE FROM THE OPEN FIRES FROM MORNING UNTIL NIGHT.

This Maasai woman is cooking for her family inside her house in Boma in the Ngong Hills of Kenya. She breathes in the fumes from the open fire all day long.

ENERGY TO COOK

In Kenya, only four per cent of the population have access to electricity. Others rely on wood and dung to burn for energy to cook and power lights to study and tools to earn a living. According to the World Health Organization (WHO), indoor smoke leads to 1.6 million deaths a year. It causes respiratory infections, lung disease, ear and eye problems, headaches, breathlessness, chest pains and giddiness. UK charity Practical Action is working with Maasai women in Kenya to develop a 'smoke hood' that reduces smoke levels in their houses by up to 80 per cent. The hood draws smoke up a chimney and outside, while drawing clean air inside through small windows. At the same time, simple changes to traditional cooking methods can also help – for example, keeping a lid on the pot to speed up the cooking process.

SOLAR COOKING

Solar cookers, which concentrate solar energy to cook food for free, are also now in use in some communities. They are particularly favoured by those living in areas where firewood is scarce – for example, in the Andes Mountains.

Solar cookers are increasingly popular with people, like this woman in Puna, northwest Argentina, who find it acceptable to cook out of doors, rather than in the privacy of their homes.

Food dyes may make our food appear more attractive and enticing, but without thorough testing, they could cause health problems.

COST OF A SNACK

Fancy a packet of crisps, a bowl of supermarket soup or a ready meal? For a few weeks in early 2005, you would probably have thought twice. A food scare was in full force after scientists detected a banned red food dye called Sudan 1 in some foods, tracing it to a batch of Worcester sauce made with contaminated chilli powder. Worries over the banned dye led to the biggest-ever recall of food products in the UK.

FOOD POLLUTION

The health risk of Sudan 1 was extremely small, according to experts. But the scare was the latest in a long line of high-profile stories from around the world about pollutants in our food. Remember the worry over **toxins** in farmed salmon? Mercury in swordfish? Benzene in soft drinks? Some of the headlines do turn into official guidelines – for example, limiting the intake of tuna for pregnant women because of potential high mercury levels. But stories about pollutants and contaminants such as Sudan 1 in our food are bound to continue to make headlines. Sudan 1 is a red dye that is used to colour non-food items such as petrol, wax and shoe and floor polish. In 2003 it became illegal to add it to food in the European Union (EU), after tests on rats showed it could cause bladder and liver cancer. So how was it spotted in the contaminated foods?

TESTING, TESTING

The UK Food Standards Agency randomly tests hundreds of imported products containing chilli every year. Any contaminated with Sudan 1 are destroyed, and all imports containing the dye have to be certified free of the additive. But officials believe that the chilli powder in question probably entered the UK before the ban came into force – only later turning up in food products.

This food researcher is collecting food extracts that are concentrated by condensation. They will be tested for pesticides and fertilizers.

INVESTIGATING THE EVIDENCE: POLLUTION IN THE ARCTIC

The investigation: It is known that concentrations of industrial chemicals and pesticides in Russians living in remote areas of the Arctic are very high. Scientists wanted to investigate how environmental pollutants in food are affecting the Inuit people of Greenland.

The scientists: A team from the Arctic Monitoring and Assessment Programme, a scientific group funded by Arctic nations, working with the Russian government and the Russian Association of Indigenous Peoples of the North.

Collecting the evidence: Doctors tested umbilical-cord blood in newborns and the breast milk of their mothers in East Greenland. They discovered high levels of contamination in large numbers of the Inuit people tested. The toxins included POPs such as PCBs, mercury, lead and cadmium.

The conclusion: The problem arises because the toxins accumulate in animals high up in the **food chain**, especially in marine mammals – a crucial part of the traditional Inuit diet. Greenland produces no significant pollution itself, so the Inuit population are suffering the effects of toxins produced elsewhere, by the world's most industrialized nations.

RUNNING INTO TROUBLE

How did you choose your last pair of trainers? Style and cost may have played a part in your decision, but pollutants probably did not. Environmental campaigner Greenpeace want to change this, with the news that most brands of trainers contain chemicals you would probably rather not wear too close to your skin.

PLASTICS PROBLEM

Phthalates are one of the key substances to watch. Added to plastics to make them more flexible, they turn up in clothes, household products – and trainers from most big manufacturers. But scientists have linked phthalates with hormonal problems in animals, and in one study, with changes to the development of the genitals of baby boys. Your wardrobe is not the only place to look for worrying environmental pollutants, according to Greenpeace. Many brands of mobile phones and computers contain so-called **brominated flame retardants**, substances that are acknowledged to be dangerous and are on their way towards being eliminated.

BAD SMELLS

In the bathroom, shampoo and shower gel often contain artificial musk, a chemical perfume that also turns up in washing powder and dishwasher tablets. As your bath water runs down the drain, it takes with it some of the perfume, releasing it into the **food chain**. Stable over long periods of time, the musk builds up – and may

Many of the chemicals found in everyday products we use around the house contain phthalates, which may cause allergies or asthma.

come back to you again at a much higher concentration in the fish you eat. The effects of artificial musk are not quite clear yet, although some studies have linked it to allergies and asthma. However, this is probably a case of what we do not know can harm us.

Computers and mobiles may contain substances that are dangerous to health.

INVESTIGATING THE EVIDENCE: PHTHALATES ALERT

The investigation: Phthalates are used in the manufacture of plastics, lubricants and solvents and are found in cosmetics, medical equipment, toys, paints and packaging. But what effect do phthalates have on human health?

The scientists: Dr Shanna Swan, director of the Center for Reproductive Epidemiology at the University of Rochester, New York, USA, and her team.

Collecting the evidence: Having found abnormalities in laboratory animals that had been exposed to phthalates, the scientists examined 134 baby boys and also tested their mothers for phthalate levels in their blood and urine.

The conclusion: Dr Swan says that, while children are sensitive to the chemicals, they are not as sensitive as the foetus. Boys born to women with higher phthalate levels were more likely to have abnormalities in their genital development. The reason for this may be that phthalates suppress the production of testosterone, which is the principal male sex hormone.

CHAPTER SIX

A STAR IS BORN

ONE NIGHT, JAY MCNEIL, A STARGAZER IN KENTUCKY, USA, LOOKED THROUGH HIS HOME TELESCOPE AND SAW A NEW STAR. IT WAS IN THE CONSTELLATION ORION, ALONGSIDE A GAS CLOUD HE HAD LOOKED AT HUNDREDS OF TIMES BEFORE. NEWS OF HIS DISCOVERY SPREAD TO THE ASTRONOMY COMMUNITY AT THE UNIVERSITY OF HAWAII, WHERE EXPERTS CONFIRMED IT USING THE COLOSSAL 8M TELESCOPE.

LIGHTS BLOCK STARRY NIGHTS

Experts are now warning that if you want to see the stars, you had better look now. Astronomy using ground-based telescopes of any size may not be possible in 40 years because of different types of pollution.

It is impossible to see the stars in our galaxy, the Milky Way, from 90 per cent of the UK. All but the brightest stars are invisible because of light pollution – the light from street lamps, security lights and any other source that, rather than focusing usefully downwards, points wastefully up. The light reflects off the atmosphere, so that when you look up, your eyes adjust to the extra light, so you cannot see the faint light from the stars.

MORE CLOUDS

The condensation trails from aircraft are also to blame, according to the latest reports. They spread out and become indistinguishable from other view-blocking clouds. At the same time, climate change is contributing to increased cloud cover that makes it impossible to spot the stars from the Earth's surface. Increasing light pollution, cheap air travel and climate change mean any clearer areas – for example, on mountain tops – may soon be under threat.

Astronomers site their telescopes in areas of the world where they are likely to find the clearest, darkest skies and the least overhead cloud cover, like these on Mauna Kea in Hawaii.

45

SAVE THE WHALES

When more than 150 whales beached themselves on the coast of western Australian in June 2005, the country's government put out a call to local residents to help. People flocked to save the whales, following official guidelines to 'keep the whales wet, and quiet'. Volunteers surrounded each whale, calming it and even giving a massage to keep the animal's circulation going, before pushing each creature out to sea. In the end, only one whale was reported to have died.

Volunteers work to rescue beached whales on a beach at Farewell Spit on South Island, New Zealand, in 2005.

NOISE LINKED TO STRANDINGS

What caused this mass stranding? One theory says that this whale species – known as the false killer whale, and technically a type of dolphin – is highly sociable. When one member of a family group is ill and heads for the shore, its relatives will follow to protect it. But there is also a theory that noise pollution is to blame. Whales communicate and navigate with sound, using a highly developed echolocation system that allows them to 'see with sound' underwater. The trouble is, the sea is getting to be a noisy place. Military operations, exploration for oil and gas and even the sound of jet skis and

Loud jet skis contribute to the noise pollution that may affect marine animals, including whales.

motorboats add up. Some studies have linked noisy activity with strandings of whales and dolphins.

NOISE POLLUTION

On dry land, sound affects us all. Noise can be hard to escape, and in many countries there are legal safeguards intended to restrict noise to reasonable levels and timescales. Inevitably, different people interpret noise pollution differently – one person's favourite record can be another person's terrible din.

INVESTIGATING THE EVIDENCE: CLASSROOM NOISE POLLUTION

The investigation: Investigations have been conducted into the effects of air pollution, lead and chemicals on children. However, until recently, no-one had looked at the effects of noise pollution, particularly if the children's schools are sited near airports. A scientific team investigated how children's learning is affected by aircraft noise.

The scientists: An international scientific team, including Barts Hospital in the UK, the Karolinska Institute and Gothenburg and Gävle universities in Sweden, RIVM in the Netherlands and CSIC in Spain.

Collecting the evidence: The team looked at data gathered from more than 2,800 children aged nine and ten living near Heathrow Airport in the UK, and airports in Spain and the Netherlands. They tested the children and used questionnaires answered by the children and their parents.

The conclusion: The team found that each five-decibel increase in noise level was linked to children being up to two months behind in their reading age. One reason may be that children learn to tune out noise pollution, but end up tuning out important noise, such as instructions from the teacher.

RADIATION AND CONTAMINATION

Today, the city of Chernobyl in northern Ukraine is a ghost town. Its population was evacuated following the worst-ever nuclear accident the world has experienced. The nuclear power plant nearby exploded on 26 April 1986, releasing clouds of radiation and leaking radioactive matter. Over the following weeks, a plume of radioactive pollution drifted over the western Soviet Union and Eastern Europe, eventually reaching the eastern USA. Serious contamination occurred in Ukraine, Belarus and Russia, and 200,000 people had to be resettled.

IMPACT THEN AND NOW

In 2005, a report by the International Atomic Energy Authority gave the toll of this accident as 56 direct deaths – 47 of the emergency workers, plus nine children who have since died of thyroid cancer. It also estimates that 4,000 people may ultimately die from illnesses related to the accident. Some campaigners believe this figure is much too low. Radiation causes damage to human tissue through its ability to **ionize** atoms and molecules – knocking electrons out of their orbits. The health effects can be extremely serious if the dose is high. Radiation destroys the ability of cells to reproduce. At a high exposure such as that produced by the Chernobyl accident, a person's bone marrow will be destroyed and other fast-growing cells, such as those in the stomach, damaged beyond repair.

RADIOACTIVE POLLUTANTS

Some exposure to radiation in ordinary life is inevitable. You might receive X-rays during medical or dental treatment. When you fly in an aircraft, you are exposed to radiation from cosmic rays.

The core of Reactor 4 at Chernobyl is shown being covered to prevent further release of radioactive contamination from the damaged reactor.

INVESTIGATING THE EVIDENCE: LOBSTERS AND NUCLEAR POLLUTION

The investigation: Sellafield Nuclear Reprocessing plant on the west coast of England used to be known as Windscale. It was notorious for being the site of the world's first big nuclear accident, which took place in October 1957. But how much radioactive waste does Sellafield discharge into the Irish Sea today, and how does this affect Ireland and the Isle of Man?

The scientists: A team from the Isle of Man's Department of Local Government and the Environment.

Collecting the evidence: The team of scientists carried out radiation monitoring of seafood, milk and meat products produced locally.

The conclusion: Lobsters caught in the Irish Sea are contaminated with the radioactive substance technetium-99, a by-product of processing old fuel rods. But the levels are now at half the peak found in 1998. Sellafield has announced the development of a new process for cleaning up some nuclear waste in order to remove technetium-99 altogether.

But people living near the Sellafield nuclear reprocessing plant in the UK have less choice about their exposure. Recent official reports say that tests on local seafood, milk and meat show contamination from Sellafield, but not at a hazardous level (see right).

Lobsters were among seafood that was tested for the effects of radioactive leakage from Sellafield.

CHAPTER SEVEN

HURRICANE DEVASTATES NEW ORLEANS

IN LATE AUGUST 2005, HURRICANE KATRINA BROUGHT DEVASTATION TO THE SOUTHERN CITY OF NEW ORLEANS, LOUISIANA, IN THE USA. HUNDREDS OF PEOPLE DIED AS FLOODS SWEPT ACROSS 80 PER CENT OF THE CITY. SIX MONTHS LATER, ALTHOUGH THE TRADITIONAL MARDI GRAS CELEBRATIONS TOOK PLACE, VAST NEIGHBOURHOODS OF THE CITY WERE STILL UNINHABITABLE, AND AN ESTIMATED 50 MILLION CUBIC METRES OF DEBRIS AND RUBBISH LINED THE STREETS.

CLIMATE CHANGE AND STRONGER HURRICANES

A study by US scientists has shown that serious storms have become twice as frequent over the past 35 years. Powerful hurricanes such as Katrina are part of a pattern of freak weather events that can only be explained by climate change, according to the latest thinking.

GREENHOUSE GASES

Experts believe that greenhouse-gas emissions are to blame for the changes in our climate. The greenhouse effect is a natural process by which our atmosphere traps the Sun's energy to warm the Earth and support life. But increases in emissions of carbon dioxide and other polluting gases artificially increase this effect. Fossil-fuel burning, in power stations fuelled by coal, oil and gas, is a major culprit. Unless we control our future greenhouse-gas output, severe weather will continue to worsen. Flooding is a severe risk to people across the planet, with 300 million people living within five metres of sea level. The UK's sea levels could rise by over 11m by the year 3000, according to climate models commissioned by the UK's Environment Agency.

Villagers in India collect food parcels dropped by an Indian air-force helicopter in 2005 after heavy rains and floods killed 300 people.

CORALS AT RISK

Coral reefs are incredible natural phenomena, living landscapes of shape and colour in crystal clear seas. But marine experts believe that climate change could consign coral reefs to history in the next 50 years. Studies show that the seas are getting warmer and more and more acidic. This process stops corals from developing – and the greenhouse gas carbon dioxide is to blame.

THE CARBON CYCLE

Normally, there is a natural balance between the carbon dioxide that is released and absorbed by the sea, the plants and the atmosphere. The carbon that is released as the plants rot away, for example, is absorbed by other plants as they grow. But humans upset the balance when they burn huge amounts of fossil fuels and release additional carbon into the atmosphere. Scientists estimate that the sea has soaked up about half the 800 billion tonnes of carbon dioxide emitted by human activity (mainly through the burning of trees, coal, gas and oil) since the start of the Industrial Revolution about 200 years ago. The carbon dioxide reacts with sea water to produce a weak acid. And because carbon dioxide levels have increased, so has the acidity. The oceans have previously recorded an 8.2 pH reading (where 7 is pH neutral, and lower numbers are more acidic). This has now dropped to 8.1 and could fall to 7.7 by the end of this century. This is the biggest and fastest decrease in pH that animals and plants that live in the sea have experienced for about 20 million years.

NO MORE COD AND CHIPS?

One of the chemical effects of a more acidic sea is the difficulty for corals and other hard-shelled creatures to get the calcium carbonate they need from the water to produce their skeletons and shells. So shellfish, snails, starfish, urchins and corals are all at risk, along with tiny creatures called plankton – vital food for favourite fish on our menus, such as cod.

When living coral reefs do not get the calcium carbonate that they need from the water, they die.

A CAREER IN SCIENCE

After working for 30 years in the fields of sea ecology and chemistry, Carol Turley is an expert in ocean acidification. She discovers deep-sea creatures that have adapted so well to life thousands of metres down that they cannot live anywhere else.

A DAY IN THE LIFE OF...

Carol Turley travels the world aboard research ships. Her work includes studying the habitats of sea creatures of all sizes – from microbes to fish. She is particularly concerned with the effects of more acidic oceans on microscopic plants called coccolithophores, which are important to our planet because they help to gobble up carbon dioxide and move it to the seabed.

THE SCIENTIST SAYS ...

"Oceans are becoming more acid because they are taking up carbon dioxide from the atmosphere, which has been produced by all the fossil fuel we burn. The impact on marine organisms and ecosystems is of great concern. Essentially, the oceans have been reducing the impact of climate change ... but at their own expense. Scientists all over the world are turning their attention to trying to find out what impact more acidic seas will have on the animals and plants that live there. The only way of stopping ocean acidification is to stop burning all those fossil fuels."

ENERGY-SAVING STARTS AT HOME

We can all make small changes in our lifestyles. Experts say that these would really make a difference in the fight against climate change.

POLLUTED ATMOSPHERE

However, we had better be quick! The Earth's climate is already changing. The ten hottest years on record have all occurred since 1990, and current climate models predict a rise in global temperatures of between 1.4 and 5.8°C over the next century.

Scientists believe that the greenhouse gases carbon dioxide, methane and others are to blame, because they pollute the atmosphere and disrupt natural cycles and processes. Currently, human activity leads to the release of about 6.5 billion tonnes of carbon dioxide every year. That is nine tonnes of carbon-dioxide for every man, woman and child in the UK. It is true that industry is directly accountable for more emissions than people are. But 27 per cent of carbon-dioxide output in the UK can be traced directly to its citizens. And the latest reports show that the overall emission levels are actually going up, not down.

Think twice before flying off to exotic locations for your holidays. You could investigate carbon offsetting (see column right) to remain climate neutral.

▶▶ www.jpmorganclimatecare.com/

MAKE A DIFFERENCE

So, what can we do? If half a million people each replaced one light bulb with an energy-efficient model, an amazing 240 tonnes of carbon-dioxide emissions could be saved. By choosing to holiday at home instead of jetting off abroad, you could make even more difference. Emissions from aircraft and ships entering and leaving Europe have more than doubled since 1990 and may double again within a decade.

The carbon dioxide released into the atmosphere by only one person in the UK every year is equivalent to five hot-air balloons' full!

A CAREER IN SCIENCE

Nicola Scholfield studied ecology and then gained a masters degree in leadership for sustainable development. Now she works for a company called Climate Care, in the UK which specializes in 'offsetting' greenhouse gas emissions. Offsetting means paying someone to reduce gases such as CO_2 in the Earth's atmosphere by the same amount that their activities add.

A DAY IN THE LIFE OF ...

Nicola Scholfield manages relationships with Climate Care's clients, selling them carbon offsets to make their business and personal activities climate neutral. Climate Care then uses the funds to support projects around the world in renewable energy, energy efficiency and forest restoration.

THE SCIENTIST SAYS ...

Nicola Scholfield believes in making her own activities carbon neutral: "I try to reduce my emissions where I can. I usually cycle or take the train to get around, and think about my energy use at home. We're planning a trip to Australia next year, and I plan to offset the emissions for our air travel."

CHAPTER EIGHT

POLLUTION BUSTING

THEY MAY LOOK LIKE ORDINARY PAVING SLABS, BUT IN REALITY THEY ARE THE LATEST TOOL IN THE FIGHT AGAINST URBAN POLLUTION. PAVING SLABS CAN REDUCE POLLUTION LEVELS BY UP TO 70 PER CENT. THE TOP LAYER CONTAINS **NANO**PARTICLES OF TITANIUM DIOXIDE THAT REACT WITH NITROGEN DIOXIDE IN POLLUTED RUSH-HOUR AIR, BREAKING IT DOWN INTO HARMLESS SALTS. IT IS THE SAME TECHNOLOGY IN ANTIBACTERIAL PAINT THAT CAN KEEP GERMS AT BAY IN HOSPITALS AND SCHOOLS.

HI-TECH MEETS LOW-TECH

Scientists and inventors continually develop ingenious ways to tackle global pollution. Researchers in California, USA, are tackling air pollution using a combined hi-tech and low-tech approach. They are recruiting 20 pigeons and giving them each a tiny backpack containing detectors, GPS location equipment and mobile phone technology. As the birds fly around the California skies, the team collects data on air quality, and this is automatically beamed back to a web page.

NOT A SCIENTIFIC ISSUE ALONE

Although hundreds of experts are devoted to monitoring and dealing with pollution and its problems, we cannot leave all the work to them. Our choices directly affect the scale of the pollution problem on our planet, and our commitment to helping find solutions to the problem is crucial.

As traffic increases on our roads, so do the problems that it brings with it. It is vital to find ways to neutralize or reduce the pollution.

The SunStang solar vehicle (powered by sunlight) takes part in the 2007 World Solar Challenge event held every year from Darwin to Adelaide, over 3,021km of Australian outback.

SILENT RIDE

If you wait for a bus in Reykjavik, Iceland, do not be surprised if the bus creeps up when you are not looking. The city's new bus fleet travels almost silently, because it is powered not by diesel, but by hydrogen. Each vehicle carries liquid hydrogen in a roof tank, which it fills at the world's first commercial hydrogen filling station. The hydrogen mixes with oxygen in a fuel cell to produce electricity, and the only exhaust is water vapour.

HYDROGEN ECONOMY

Electric vehicles often call to mind the trusty milk float – a quiet form of transport, but not one that is known for its speed or long range. However, Iceland's fuel-cell buses can travel up to 200km on a tank of fuel, and have a top speed of 105km/h. Their launch in Reykjavik is part of the country's aim to become the first world economy independent of fossil fuels – an aim that should mean an enormous reduction in their pollution output too. Traffic pollution is responsible for a host of problems, including the emission of health-damaging fumes and particles and planet-damaging gases. Campaigns to reduce our dependence on cars focus on car sharing (there are ten million empty seats

▶▶ www.wsc.org.au/

on the roads every day, as cars travel with only one or two people on board), or leaving the car at home for short journeys.

THE HYBRID CAR IS GREENER

Scientists are working on ways to make vehicles more sustainable and less polluting when we do need to use them. One of the most advanced inventions so far is the hybrid engine that combines petrol power with an electric motor. When you are travelling more slowly in town, the car uses its motor – a quiet option and one that produces almost no pollution at all. The petrol engine kicks in at higher speeds at which it can run more efficiently, and when the driver brakes, on-board systems charge the battery.

This Icelandic bus is powered by hydrogen gas, which is much cleaner and cheaper than conventional fossil fuels.

INVESTIGATING THE EVIDENCE: SOLAR-POWERED CAR WINS 2005 RACE

The investigation: In 2005, a team built a solar-powered car, Nuna III. The third in a series, they wanted to test how fast a car can travel when powered only by clean solar energy.

The scientists: Students at the Delft University of Technology in the Netherlands.

Collecting the evidence: The team used the hi-tech laboratories and workshops of the university to develop Nuna III. They then entered the car in the 2005 World Solar Challenge, a 3,021-km race held nine times over the last 20 years across the outback between the cities of Darwin and Adelaide, Australia. The race attracts inventors and competitors from all over the world. Nuna III won the race at an overall average speed of 103km/h – an improvement of 6km/h over the record achieved in 2003.

The conclusion: Nuna III proved that speed is no problem for a car powered by solar cells. Now the challenge is to build a new generation of solar cars that can be easily modified for everyone to drive.

BLACKOUT CRISIS

California in the USA is a seemingly wealthy state and home
to the innovative hi-tech companies of Silicon Valley, including
DreamWorks Animation and Google. But in 2001, it came as
a shock to the state's population that there were a series of
blackouts as engineers struggled to meet demand for power.
Authorities blamed supply problems as people switched on
their energy-hungry air-conditioning units.

FOSSIL FUELS ARE RUNNING OUT

In the past 100 years, people have learned to rely on electricity
for cooking, communication, entertainment and much more
in their everyday lives. Most of the power comes from burning
fossil fuels, and this causes huge pollution problems and the
risk of disaster when reserves run out, as they will. Current
forecasts show there are less than 100 years of gas and oil
reserves, and less than 200 years of coal. Across Europe,
it is already possible to choose an electricity supplier that

uses cleaner power sources than the traditional coal, oil and gas. Companies either sell electricity that has been generated using 'green' sources, or contribute to a fund that is developing new and renewable energy projects. Wind power, solar energy, water power and **biomass** (animal dung or vegetable oil) are all 'green' sources.

CLEAN COAL

In developing economies such as China and India, however, coal is a key fuel for the power stations that are springing up. New clean coal technology could mean greener power, using a process in which coal is turned into a gas before it is burned efficiently, and the resulting gases collected for storage. Whatever happens, people need to develop not only new sources of power, but also new ways of living their lives.

In Iceland, people bathe at the Blue Lagoon spa, which is fed by the water output from a nearby geothermal power plant. Superheated water from the ground near a lava flow is used to run turbines that generate electricity.

acid rain rain, snow or sleet that contains concentrations of acid-forming chemicals

biomass the mass of all biological organisms, dead or alive, apart from that changed into substances such as coal or petroleum. Biomass is often burned as a fuel

brominated flame retardant a chemical that is added to plastics to guard against fire. They are known to build up in the environment

carbon dioxide a greenhouse gas emitted when fossil fuels burn

carbon monoxide a gas that has no taste or smell, but is highly toxic

chlorofluorocarbons (CFCs) a group of gases containing carbon, that are used in products such as fridges and air-conditioning units

chromosome a structure in all living cells that carries the genes that determine cell function

climate change a long-term significant change in weather patterns that can be natural or caused by the activities of people

dioxin an organic chemical that is released into the air in both natural events such as forest fires and by incineration of waste. Dioxins are also toxic by-products when many items are manufactured

Envisat Europe's biggest and most expensive satellite, carrying sensitive scientific instruments for monitoring the environment

food chain a term for a series of organisms where each species is eaten in turn by another

fossil fuel a non-renewable material formed over millions of years, such as oil, coal or natural gas, that can be burned and used for energy

genetically modified describes a living organism when its genetic material has been altered to give it different characteristics

global warming an increase in the average temperature of the Earth that may cause climate change

greenhouse gas a gas, such as carbon dioxide, that traps heat from the Sun in the Earth's atmosphere

ice core a sample taken by scientists from the accumulation of snow and ice over many years

Industrial Revolution a huge social and technological change in Britain between about 1760 and 1830, when machinery took over from manual labour

ionize to separate or change into ions (electrically charged atoms or group of atoms)

methane a greenhouse gas that is emitted when fossil fuels burn

nano short for nanotechnology which describes science and technology taking place on a nano scale, that is between 0.1 and 100nm. One nanometer equals one-thousandth of a micrometre or one-millionth of a millimetre

nitric oxides a group of gases given off by burning petrol. Although harmless by themselves, they react to form nitrogen dioxide, which irritates people's lungs and airways.

nutrient a source of nourishment

ozone a molecule of three oxygen atoms present in the Earth's atmosphere. At ground level it is an air pollutant, and in the upper atmosphere (the ozone layer) it protects the Earth from damaging ultraviolet radiation

ozonesonde a lightweight, balloon-borne instrument that meteorologists use to measure pressure, temperature and humidity in the atmosphere

particulate matter how scientists refer to extremely tiny particles, some of which occur naturally from volcanoes, dust storms, fires and sea spray, but also in large quantities from burned fossil fuels

peat organic matter found in marshy or damp regions. Peat is cut and dried for use as a fuel

pesticide a chemical used by farmers for destroying plant, fungal or animal pests

pH value a chemical value that is used to describe the acidity or alkalinity of something

phthalate a chemical that is added to plastics to make them more flexible

POPs (persistant organic pollutants) a group of stable, artificial organic chemicals, mostly developed for use in industry, that build up in the environment

radiation the emission of heat and light, transmitted as rays

Sciamachy one of the monitoring instruments aboard Envisat

sediment material that settles on the bottom of streams, lakes and seas

smog 'smoky fog' or 'sooty fog' that occurs in still, polluted conditions

toxic poisonous; capable of causing death or injury

toxin a poison produced by a living organism or an industrial process